Tips for being a successful leader. Warning if you do not want to be the very best you can be in management or supervision do not read this book. If you are not in management or supervision or intend to be in the management or supervisory position do not read this book. It contains things that you will not understand!

Introduction

I'm writing this book to better help people know and understand what it is to be a leader and how to have leadership skills. But the best way to understand leadership, first you have to understand what leadership is and why leadership is needed. In addition to meeting certain criteria to even be considered as a leader. Throughout this book, I will be giving you multiple explanations, examples do's and don'ts along with traits that a leader should and should not have. I will give you examples and scenarios for each trait that a leader should have detailed trait by trait. I will explain how each one is necessary and what it looks like when you have mastered that certain trait. I will also explain what happens if you don't understand a certain trait and where it is needed and necessary to be considered a great leader. Leadership is like a recipe, you have to have the right ingredients along with the right recipe, anybody can bake a cake. If you follow the directions and use the ingredients as called for in the recipe, the cake will come out the same. If you tweak an ingredient here or there you will not get the same result, you will not get the perfect cake. What I am giving you is a recipe for the perfect cake, whether you follow these directions or not is up to you. After all, when you are done with it you will be the one who eats the cake. My goal is for you to better understand how to become a great leader and what you should look for in your staff to become great leaders. After all, everyone wants to be led they just don't want to be led to slaughter.

Drive

The first ingredient is drive. Why is drive so important? Leading people is a very tenuous endeavor, you have to have the drive to move and motivate people into getting things done. If you do not have the drive nor the motivation to do things, things will not get done. You cannot ensure that the vision that you want for the people that you lead is being carried out on a daily basis, if you don't have the drive to engage them. Having this drive is not easy, to train yourself to do this you can start small, by setting a routine for yourself.

Example 1 set bookmarks for yourself every day. It can be as simple as making your bed every day, or going for a walk. Anything that has you repeating the same routine every day. What this does is condition yourself to a routine and follow through so that it doesn't seem like a task but more like the norm .It's getting in to your car and putting on your seatbelt, it's just something you do, even though it's the law, you do it anyway because you have established that routine. There are people who don't put on their seatbelts not because they want to break the law, but because they have set a routine of not Buckling up. When you are a leader there are lots of checks and balances. To do so you will need to have the drive to do the checks so that everything balances out.

Accomplishments

Whatever field that you're trying to be a leader in you have to accomplish something. The one thing that people do to their leaders on a daily basis is challenge their leadership. Example, how many times have you gone to work and thought about your boss. Wondering to yourself how did they ever get his/her job, or he/her doesn't do anything, or I can do this job better than him/her, or they only got this job because they knew someone. That line of thinking is a major hurdle for leaders to overcome because every decision that you make will be second-guessed and critiqued by the people left to carry out your orders. The only way to overcome that obstacle is to accomplish things in whatever field that you're working. You have to accomplish something, meaning your past accomplishments will speak for you when you're not speaking. Your accomplishments will be there to defend you when you're not there to defend yourself. Now don't get me wrong, I'm not asking you to build rockets and send people to the moon or balance the budget or win five championships. Accomplishments can be something as small as being an employee of the month for a few months in a row, having perfect attendance always being on time or just being a person in the clutch that everyone can count on. If you want to lead a group of people in a certain field the best way to do that is survey the people around, know what all of their weaknesses are, and be better than everyone else or one or two of them. Example; if you work around 10 employees and eight of them are always late missing work, that means that things are not getting done on time deadlines are not being met, which leaves holes that will need to be filled. The average person would look at that situation and just get frustrated and say oh well I work with a bunch of lazy people and just deal with it. That mind frame is not the mind frame a leader. A leader looks at that situation and sees ways that he/she can accomplish goals for him/her by being on time, always come to work, and learn the responsibilities of the people who don't show up for work and do their job, so that things get done. When that happens you easily separate yourself from the pack. In time you become the go-to person who knows everything and was always there that's an accomplishment. So when the day finally comes for you to get a promotion. You get the raise and no one can second-guess the decision since you have accomplished so much by coming to work on time, having a great attendance record and learning everyone else's job and filling those holes so that things get done. That person has put themselves in a position to grow and become a leader without saying anything but making accomplishments. People talk about that person and their accomplishments. Build on that and keep accomplishing things and congrats to that guy or gal they are about to get his or her first leadership position.

Controversy

Controversy is good sometimes you need an opening to make changes. Controversy (or strife) can be the catalyst for change or people will go on with the same old same old knowing that there are problems that need to be fixed, but have no reason to fix them. Controversy opens the door for that change and start the dialogue or discussion. It allows the conversation to start so that change can be made, there is a lot of good things that come from controversy. Example I live in the Washington D.C. area and we have a transit system called the Metro system. This went on for years and years under certain leadership with faulty maintenance records untrained staff, and a culture of passing the buck. Which lead to a series of accidents and deaths. This controversy helped change the culture and held people accountable to get things fixed for the better.

Sometimes people don't change unless they have to. So, if you use controversy wisely you can use it as a tool to get things you want to see fixed in your area of expertise or in your job.

The five kinds of leaders

No matter what area of expertise you're in or whatever kind of job you have most leaders fall into five categories. Firefighter, the warden, the last man standing, the babysitter and the coach. I will explain each category and I guarantee you know someone who falls into one of these or maybe even yourself.

The Firefighter

The firefighter is a person that chases his/her problems trying to fix one problem after the next, but with no permanent solution to fix the problem. They spend half of the day if not all jumping from issue to issue. Lots of times it is the same issue because he did not fix it previously. The firefighter also sees problems, never fixes them just so he could act like the one that's coming to the rescue. To me, these people are dangerous to an organization because they let things fester without totally fixing them just so they can have the glory of saving the day.

The Warden

The Warden is a person who is a stickler for the rules, no matter how small or big the infraction he will enforce it. He will bury you in paper and is always reprimanding an employee for any infraction that he might see. He rules with the employee guidebook this kind of person is also dangerous. Yes, rules are needed but they are guidelines to keep things in check. Not to rule over people with no sense of judgment or temperament. When you don't have anything else to stand on far as leadership skills, this person always relies on, the employee handbook rule book, or contract  because they have no other way of focusing or mentoring to fix issues.

The Last man standing

The last man standing is it interesting fellow, he's been around for years and the job fell into his lap because no one else wanted to do it. He/she has been there so long that it was put on him. He should know everything he has seen everything, he/she is the defacto leader. He/she doesn't really want the job, or can't really do the job because he/she is lacking people skills, has no problem-solving skills, and maybe even zero motivation skills. He/she has a job just because no one else wants it that's why he's the last man standing

The Babysitter

The Babysitter is a person who just needed a job, might have the degree in a certain field to be a supervisor or manager. He/she might know somebody who gave him or her the job but doesn't really care about bettering people. This person doesn't really care about accomplishing the mission at hand, just is a translator from the upper management to the employees. They don't want to fix any issues and actually doesn't really care about any issues. He/she is just there because the supervisor needs to be there. Somebody has to do the write ups, somebody has to be there to answer the questions, somebody has to open the building, somebody has to set the alarm, he or she is there to watch over the employees until it's time to go home.

The Coach

The coach is the guy generally trying to get the best out of his employees. Whether they are the fastest or slowest, the most intelligent or the least intelligent, the tallest or shortest, the sharpest or the dullest knife. The coach is going to get the best out of that person and get the goals accomplished. He will do this by studying who you are, by putting you in a position to succeed, finding methods that cater to your skill set so you can succeed. Drawing up plans like X's and O's for each employee to put them in the right position to get task completed properly.

The coach knows exactly what he needs to say to get out of people what he needs to get done. He's the coach, always planning,always motivating, and always try to accomplish a goal.

I guarantee you know someone who falls in one of these categories or you yourself maybe in one of these categories. There is nothing wrong with any of them if in the right environment .

The five "tions"
Expectation, Communication, Motivation, Documentation Termination

These five words are a managers or leaders best tools if used properly:

1.Expectation: You have to give a person or the employee a goal. You have to give them something to shoot for with a clear set of guidelines so that he/she feels as if they have accomplished something. Whether it's a task that needs to be completed on a time basis, or you need to have a certain amount of sales in a time frame and also let them know what failure looks like, also the pros and cons of a task is done properly or not.

2.Communication: You have to be very clear and accurate to make sure that what you're trying to convey to your employees. Even if through a broad spectrum of classes and backgrounds or nationalities that they understand you. If they don't understand you and you don't have a clear line of communication with them you would not be able to get anything out of them. Communication is key, they must, I repeat they must be able to understand you and be able to have a clear dialogue back and forth that each of you understands one another. That you understand and know they hear you and they have a very good understanding of what they need to accomplish .

3.Motivation: Every person is different, every person is motivated differently to do the same task. Example, you might have five people doing the same job, the exact same job but one person may be motivated to get up and go to work because he or she has to pay bills for their family, one person might be motivated to use said job as a stepping stone to go to another job, one person may be motivated just because they need a job, and one person might be motivated because someone is pushing them out of the house to get up and go to work. I say this, because each one of these people is motivated by different factors so to get all these people that work at the same job to complete said task the same way they all need a different push in a different way to get them to complete the tasks assigned to them. Even though they may have the same task there are motivated by different things. It's up to a good leader to figure out what motivates this person. It might be the ability to want to be the best it might be the ability to not to have anyone say anything to them just let them do their job. You have to constantly give people goals no matter if it's the receptionist the guy filling orders or the salesman quotas and goals are good. If you don't have a goal, how can you score if you don't score? You can't win so no matter what your expectations are for a person, let them know exactly how much you want them to succeed.

4. Documentation. Documentation is one of the most underrated things of a manager can use but is also his or her best friend. When people tell you things and suggest things document them. A human mind can only hold so much data. It's always good to jot down notes and make a file for your employees, for yourself, or your bosses. When things are said that don't sound right or they give you the shakes or something you might not understand. jot them down so you can use them as a reference. If you have an employee that is problematic and is always saying slick things with there mouth and doing silly things document them. It's a guarantee one day all of those things that you document will come in handy when you write reviews and you want to recall a certain situation. When someone tells you something and you forgot but documented properly you can always go back to say on this date at this time this was said. This will shock and awe people documentation is the biggest gun with the biggest bullet. When it fires it rarely misses, so jot things down on the computer or notepad and train yourself to make documentation about everything. I guarantee you will have a lot less issues with certain people saying things to you and asking you questions. This will give you more scenarios in which you remember what they don't remember. Document things on a continuous basis, it will prevent a lot of misgivings coming your way. People will not test you nor will they comment to you about silly games if they know you always document things, When they know you're a person that jots down everything you'll be surprised about how many problems don't come your way. People will always try to pass the buck, put their problems off on people to set people up but, when they know you document things they don't even try.

documentation makes you **STRONG**

5.Termination:

Termination is a thing that an owner, leader, or manager will have to do from time to time. If done properly, termination can be a good thing. It cuts the weeds from the grass but without proper documentation, you won't know which weed needs cutting. To be honest most employees terminate themselves for lack of work lack of completing tasks, lousy attendance, and poor work ethic.You, as the leader, just have to give them the bad news but be honest with them.

Putting all five of these words together in your daily life will make it easy for you to navigate the daily trials of being a good leader.

Meetings

Meetings are a very important tool in management. If used correctly meetings give you a chance to express the views that you have to your employees and that also gives you a form in which you can look them in the eye. You can communicate to them and this lets you gauge who's paying attention who was asleep at the wheel, and who was really excited to hear your voice over distracted. If done correctly it gives you a chance to know who needs extra attention. You should have meetings every day at the start of your day (whenever that may be), or before starting a major task. This is the time to express whatever your feeling about the task at hand to your employees. Tell them what success looks like and what failure looks like how to accomplish the goals at hand and how to avoid failing. The number one answer when things go wrong employees use is "I did not know" or "I do not understand" or "no one told me". They're all the same answer just phrased different. When you have meetings you negate those answers. One thing I recommend doing in a meeting is to give some kind of life lesson or philosophy. This lets your employees know that you are intellectually engaged with them and shows a sense of caring. That you would like to enlighten their minds and some kind of way and always end the meeting with this phrase. Does anybody have any questions comments or concerns? Does everybody know what is asked of them? Does everybody know what to do? "Let's have a safe and productive day".

Your Voice

Your employees need to hear your voice. What I mean by that is the need to always hear the tone of your voice. The tone of your voice speaks a lot when you're serious and you're trying to give out information to your employees. They need to know what your saying and your tone tells them that you are serious or not too serious. Whatever the case may be your employees need to be use to hearing the tone of your voice in each situation. This would help your employees to differentiate and prioritize what you are telling them. Always try to communicate as much as possible and let your employees hear your voice and your change in vocal tones this will go a long way in helping to translate to each one of them. Example, even if an employee does not speak perfect english, whatever language you're speaking, speak in a certain tone will let them know that whatever you're saying is serious or if it is to be taken in a playful manner.

Not too Friendly

Never be too friendly with your employees. Don't get me wrong, there is nothing wrong with being friends with your inner circle, your right hand man / woman or a member of management to help you get things done. Your employees or staff need to view you in a position of strength, not of playfulness. By giving the impression that you are all business all the time even, if that's not the case. When you are too friendly with your employees, they get a false sense of security. They get the impression that they can do things like, miss deadlines, not be as focused as they should be because you will not not take their failure to heart. That is a grave injustice to your company that you work for. I'm not saying try to be a moron all the time, but they have to view you as a person that takes the company seriously and if needed be very aggressive when the time calls for it. A good leader is the balance between right and wrong, good and bad, and equality and inequality. At the end of the day your employees will only go as far as they think you would let them go.

K.I.S.S.

Keep It Simple Stupid

I'm told that it's a military phrase but this is one of the most truthful phrases I've ever heard. The one mistake that businesses make time and time again is over complicate processes. The best processes when you look at them are the most simple processes. There is a saying the quickest way to one point to another is a straight line. Most businesses create a lot of processes ,procedures and policies to govern the way their businesses run, Big mistake. That's because no matter how many processes, procedures, or policies you have, you need people to implement them and like most people we gravitate to things that are simple and not complicated. So when you're making your policies and procedures just remember there is a person at the other end of it to make it work. The easier you make that policy or procedure the better chance you have that policy or procedure will be met or have It's affected goal.

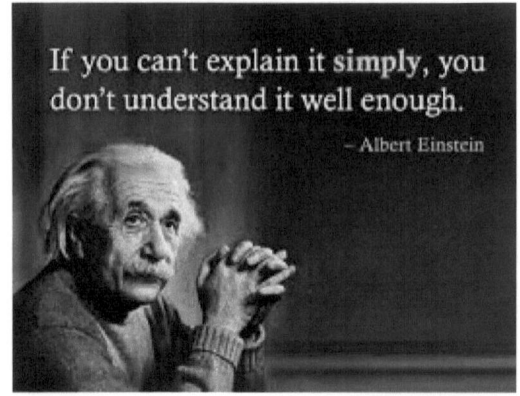

Inner Circle

It is important for any good manager or supervisor or CEO to have a strong inner circle. When I say inner circle, I do not mean supervisors, managers or VPs. I mean people in different areas and branches that you might not normally think would be in a CEO or managers inner circle. I will give you an example, you could be a manager of the company, you can have a cashier, a stockroom clerk or a driver. All of these guys can be in your inner circle because they don't want to be VPs and managers. They want to do the jobs they do and be comfortable. But you can also use these people to give you vital information. Straight from the front lines that you can use to better navigate through your company. No one has to know who is in your inner circle they don't even have to know each other. That's why it's called your inner circle. Each one of these people has valuable Intel on how your company runs. As a whole, the driver sees the interaction with the customers and how the orders are pulled and is loaded on one trucks. The stock guy could tell you how inventory is being maintained and how the managers and supervisors running the warehouse or store. They can also help with the interactions that are seen by the employees. A secretary could tell you the gossip in the office. All of these things are vital to the decision-making process. When you have enough information to make the right decision you will make the right one and where you get the data from is crucial. You inner circle doesn't have to go to dinner with you or even play golf with you. You can reward them in your own way. It's best to have one-on-one relationships with your inner circle, so they can feel as though they are part of something and always try to reward them accordingly on the stature of which they deserve.

The Looks Of Things

Try to make sure that you pay a lot of attention to the details a.k.a. the little things. When you pay attention to the little things it trains your eyes to look at the Subtleties of things. If you only look at the big picture you lose sight of all the little ins and outs. They slip past you and if enough little things slip past you they can form into a major big thing. This is why it's always important to sweat the little things whether it's the symmetric view of the aisles (if you're in a retail store), the cleanliness of your floors,the appearance of your employees and your trucks. Everything matters, there is always someone somewhere who is paying attention to the little things and as a manager when you pay attention to the little things it lets your subordinates below you know that they need to pay attention to the little things also.First impressions mean a lot, you never get those back. If you set a high first impression, people have a tendency to hold you to an even higher standard and when everybody knows there is a high standard to be held up to they will eventually give the extra effort to reach that higher standard.Your attention to detail and being a stickler for the little things lets your employees know that everything matters to you. One thing that I know for sure if you cannot do the little things right, you definitely will miss the big
things.

P.A.S.
(People Are Stupid)

Yep, you heard me **people are stupid**! Okay, now let me explain. A person is and considered smart by going to an Ivy League school and having degrees, and generally good knowledge of whatever field he or she is in. Let's look at the average everyday person, your employees. Where do they get their knowledge from? Where did he or she get the understanding of what they have to do in the everyday job functions? Just like you are what you eat and you are what you know. If a person gets their information from reliable sources like books, Encyclopedias, maybe a certain news organization, or maybe just from their friends. If a person's knowledge comes from bad places than their understanding of things is bad, which makes them stupid people that will believe anything they hear or see. So depending upon the sources that they get the information from they might not be very knowledgeable. This is a must to remember you really need to understand this when you look at people that you cannot just automatically think everybody should know this particular issue because it's common sense, sorry it doesn't work that way. People do what they know, it's up to you as a manager or supervisor to constantly educate your employees so that they know what you want them to know because the decisions that they make when you're not around will govern how your company is run. The best things you can do is make sure that that knowledge that you want your employees to have is instilled into them own a daily basis from the sources that you want them to receive it from. This is very, very crucial especially to the success of your business. Never overestimate your employees expectations if you have not put the time into them to guarantee that they are educated towards the goals they are trying to accomplish. I hate to say it but you always must assume that people are stupid! Because they can make an **ASS** out of **U** and **ME.**

Trust And Verify

Micromanaging is never a good thing especially when your employees notice it. As a good leader it is up to you to translate what needs to be done to your employees and give them the tools and training necessary to do it. By giving them a sense of trust, this will enhance the bond between the employee and the leader. You must always have a way to verify that the job or task they have been entrusted to is being done to your specifications without looking over their shoulder. This could be accomplished in many different ways. Example, someone else could do it and report back to you, it's always good to have good subordinates or some kind of computer program that you can access to verify the task is done correctly. Set certain benchmarks or deadlines that will trigger something that you can easily see, the more your employees know you have trust in them the better job they will do. Yet always have a way to verify if a tasks is not completed correctly. When a task is not completed correctly always counsel employees by letting them know exactly what went wrong by not accomplishing this task and ways to correct the problem in the future. By not looking over there shoulder and micromanaging them you give yourself and aura of see everything without actually being there,this also is effective in showing your employees that you see and are paying attention to everything.

Currency

Throughout my career in management I have always been able to make budgets or beat budgets consistently.The reason behind that success is because I treat my employees as currency. I will explain it this way to make it really easy to understand. In your life you have bills and needs weying on the money that you have, whether it's a car notes or electric bill or taking your girlfriend out on a date. You only have so much money so the trick is to balance out which you need versus which you want.The same rules apply with managing and budgeting. Always take care of your necessities things that pay the bills. If you have 10 employees on a shift and they work an eight hour shift with breaks that's seven hours per person which gives you 70 man hours for that day to accomplish your goals. You have to get in the practice of looking at your employees that way and spend those currency hours accordingly. No matter what field you are in this rule will apply. The trick is to use your currency to pay the bills that need to be paid and know what you can put on the back burner for another day. The same way you do in your normal life because at some point every bill will need to be paid after that is done you can concentrate on the things you want.

Data

The best way not to make a good decision is not to use emotion but to use good data. Whatever field you are in you have to make decisions with good info and data on all aspects of what you do. And when I say data I mean right down to the smallest detail. Example, if you are in a retail business how many customers are in your door on what days, what time of day, and what they are buying. How many employees does it take to service these customers effectively? I don't care if you work in a McDonald's and you have to break down how many burgers or Big Macs you sell. At so many points throughout the day All of that data goes to help you make good decisions about personnel and how to market your business how to manage your workflow etc. Good data is definitely one of the keys to success so I advise you to try and find a way if you don't have it already to accumulate all facets of data throughout your business. This will almost guarantee that every decision you make will be the right one.

Rewards

It's always good practice to reward your employees well when they accomplish really good deeds. Personal fulfillment is one unforeseen aspects of leadership. Nurturing that hidden aspect of people, which motivates them to be number one or be the best at what they do is complemented by an appropriate reward system, At the end of the day, no one wants to be last but everybody cannot be first, so it's good to reward those who deserve it and to make the others who don't deserve it want more and and wish that they could also have the reward. They will realize that it is obtainable because at the end of the day a person comes to work for the paycheck, they do not do a great job for the same pay,you have to have some obtainable goal for them to be able to reach, without a goal how can you score? It is also not a bad idea to single out the worst of the bunch to show separation to the rest of the employees, one of the best ways to get improvement out of an employee is peer pressure.

The Gardener

Be a good gardener, what I mean by that is think of your employees as flowers and you are the gardener. Certain flowers need sunlight, certain flowers need more watering than others, and sometime you have weeds that grow in certain gardens. You have to be the gardener that's willing to give the sunlight when it's needed, water when it's needed, and get rid of the weeds when it's needed. Sunlight can be a metaphor for knowledge water could be a metaphor for encouragement, and weeds could be a metaphor for those bad apples or employees in the bunch that you need to cut out. Mastering those skills will make you a very good leader, you got to know when to give the proper encouragement, the proper knowledge, and when to cut your losses.

The Box

There used to be an old saying ""think outside the box" that used to be, all the rage and something inventive and exciting to say you're an outside the box thinker. I found that in my 30+ years in management, that the best way of thinking is to take that box break it down, and put it in the compactor. Never limit yourself with any bound set of rules since the age of the Internet. There is no boundaries to which you can't accomplish if you put your mind to it, always think in simple terms. What are we try to accomplish? What are the boundaries preventing us from getting to point A to point B? Think of simple ways that you can get to point A to point B, find the most efficient way by using whatever you can think of to do. It's always the simplest idea that ends up being the best one. That idea people will say "man why didn't I think of that". Never limit yourself, always do research, and always listen to those around you. Find out what the real problems are and find real solutions for solving them. There is a big difference between an excuse and a reason, a reason can be explained an excuse is just that, so never limit yourself.

Unreasonable Expectations

There is a thin line between motivation and unreasonable expectations. What I mean by that is you can challenge someone by giving them hard assignments,and pushing them to fulfill their potential That's a sign of good management. You can push a person to hard and literally break them, so be careful not to give your employees too much at one time. You can take the risk of losing a very good employee if you do it wrong, remember there is nothing wrong with pushing a person but there is something wrong with pushing a person over the edge. A good manager knows how to challenge their employees aggressively without being too aggressive.

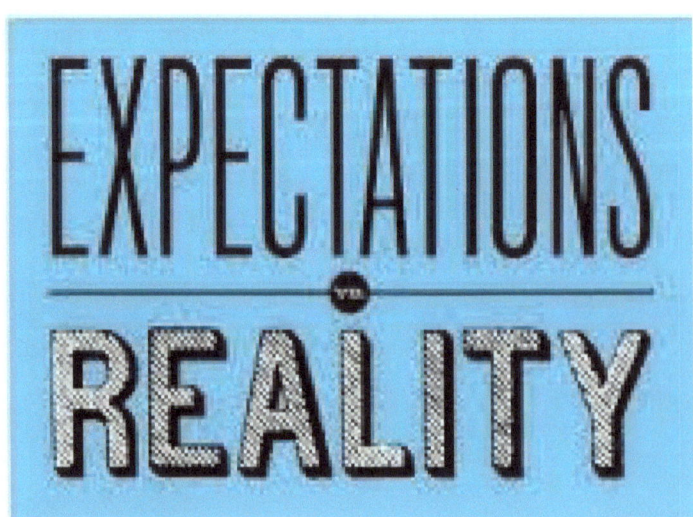

OPEN DOOR POLICY

Open-door policy is one of the oldest sayings in the book for the workplace, but what does it really mean? Most people just say it because it's something that they should say to their employees. This gives them the impression that they can come to that person for anything, sadly in most cases, that is not the case. Most managers and supervisors will play the i'm too busy not right now make an appointment card. A true open-door policy is what it was meant to be, when you are accessible whether by phone, email, or an actual open-door. Employees have a lot to say, they have a lot of ideas, and have a lot of things they want to get off their chest. Most times they will have vital information that you need, so it is important to have an open door policy and an open mind policy also. If you are a manager or supervisor that has employees in multiple divisions/areas or states, try to find a way to interact with all of your employees so that they can get to you in a confidential way. Try to make an effort to reply to their concerns, that free flow of information will pay off big time in the long run.

Respect Vs Fear

There are two basic foundations that leaders base everything they do on one's fear and the other is respect. Both are very effective but only one gets the best results in my opinion. Let's talk about fear first, you can use the fact that you can fire people, give them terrible assignments and change their work schedules etc. Fear is a very proper tool but can be used too aggressively at times and you miss out on engaging your employees and meaningful dialogue because they just don't want to talk to you. Now let's talk about respect, there are multiple ways of having people respect you but in a leadership role having people respect you for your background, your willingness to engage employees to make them better teaching them things on an continuous basis. When you've earned the respect of people they engage more and work harder for you even when you're not around because at the end of the day you're still the leader and you still can change the schedules. Give tough work assignments, discipline them and terminate them, but don't let that be your base. So in my opinion it's better to be respected than
feared.

Fear vs Respect

Fear breaks; Respect mends.
Fear hurts; Respect heals.
Fear suffocates; Respect motivates.
Fear arrests; Respect enables.

Vinod Varma

Confrontation

Dealing with confrontation can make or break the morale and the progress that you have made with your employees. Dealing with confrontation properly shows your poise and leadership skills Dealing with confrontation badly shows just the opposite. When dealing with hostile employees or people in general it's best to remember to watch your tone when talking back to them, when you speak with a civil tone that tends to start the diffusion process. Like the old saying goes" adding fuel to the fire", a civil and calm tone is like a fire extinguisher. When people are upset, they tend to speak with emotion and not reason and they are very hard to understand. This is why as a leader you must try to calm them down as quickly as possible your tone of voice will start the ball rolling in the right direction so you can actually understand what it is they are complaining about or understand the point that they are trying to make. Try as best as you can to lock in on the facts of what the problem is, most times than not It's a simple fix something that you can revert back to in the employee handbook. If that is the case simply remind them of what the policy is, if it's of a personal nature try to avoid giving advice. Most times people are just venting and want someone to hear them out. The quicker they can get what's on their chest off the quicker they will calm down,and get back to work.

Short Cuts

For every policy or procedure that can be implemented, there will be someone to find shortcuts through each process. Shortcuts are not specific to one person, people do what is the easiest for them in the boundaries that they have. That is one of the most troublesome things about policies and procedures. They always make sense to the person that has made them, and there's always somebody that can find a way around it and still accomplish the same goal. This is the beauty of human beings, we have the ability to tear down anything , and build anything. It is up to you as a leader to find ways to integrate the shortcuts into policy. This is why it is important to have a good level of communication and a good open-door policy and an open mind policy also. By listening to your employees and observing how they maneuver through policies and procedures you can better craft a perfect policy and set of procedures that is easy to follow and very efficient. Remember every play is drawn out to be a touchdown play, but it all depends on the personnel that carries out the play that will determine if its a touchdown. So always try to cater, if it's possible, your procedures and policies to the people that have to implement them.

Teachable moments

From time to time in your role as a leader, you will see things that are done totally wrong against policy or procedure and things that just don't make any sense. This will happen and will happened often despite your best efforts. What you can do to minimize them is use them as teachable moments. A teachable moment is to simply point out what a person did wrong against the policies and procedures by reminding them what the policies and procedures are. You can talk with them through the process that they have failed upon point out exactly what they did wrong. Find out as best you can what their thought process is and why they did the process wrong then give them the flaws in their thinking, revert back to the policies and explain to them this is why that policy exists in the first place. This generates a one-on-one dialogue, most often time bares good fruit and most times a teachable moment will be a situation in which you also can learn as well.

SAFETY

Safety is one of the main concerns of companies. Safety for their employee's, safety for their customer's and safety for their product. When an employee feels safe in the work environment they're more likely to do a better job for you. When a customer feels safe they are more likely to give you their business, and when you keep your product safe you take less losses. You must promote safety on a consistent basis with your employees it needs to be embedded into the psyche and almost become a second nature to them. This should always be a daily emphasis on safety in some form or fashion. It needs to be basic for employees to ensure safety safeguards checklists etc. Workmen's Comp. and insurance costs are staggering to a business, safety is one way to guarantee your bottom line and needs to be taken very seriously everyday. As a leader, never be afraid to correct people when they are doing something that is considered unsafe, even if you have to say it every day to until it is embedded into them. This needs to be done and sometimes it is necessary to get people who are unsafe out of your company as fast as possible.

Culture

When I talk about culture i'm not talking about race or ethnicity. I'm talking about the focus of the employees underneath your leadership, really think about the way they interact with each other the way they interact with your customers. The focus that they have to get the mission plan accomplished, i'm talking about the culture of a company moving as one with one common goal to have your vision become reality. The mark of a good leader is to be able to accomplish that. The culture of your employees shines through when they're not even thinking about it, it becomes second nature. If embedded in their psyche properly everything they do will be to accomplish the goal that you have set forth for your company. Whether it's absolute customer service, quality of products, safety or efficiency. It all starts from when you put people in close environment. They have no choice but to conform to whatever culture a real leader provides,if not they form factions among themselves. This is a clear indication that they do not know what direction they should be going, and they take leadership from the wrong places. This is not beneficial to you as a leader or your company. The culture of your company should always come from the top and work its way down. If not, people will find their own way, and nine times out of ten it will not be the way that you want them to go. So at every turn always embed into your employees what the focus is and how they should act. They need to know what it is to be an employee of the company so that it is second nature to them so, they do it without even thinking. This pays very good dividends in the long run, I have a saying " The Company's name is not the company your employees are the company".

The Test

The test of a good leader can be seen when he is not around and the operation runs smoothly. But when they say, "the cat's away and the mice will play", this shows how invested your employees are into the belief system that you have put into them. If your employees run amok and things went awry, it means that you as a leader have not invested the time into them and has done very little to integrate your will and your vision into your employees. If your employees work in a cohesive efficient manner when you're not around, it shows that you have done a very good job in integrating your will into the psyche. The greatest mark of a good leader is how your employees act when you're not around, this shows that you have trained each individual person under your tenure to operate in a certain manner they know the focus, the direction, and they know the focus without even thinking because you have put the work in them to ensure that they know exactly what they are doing. If they know that you're not around they will want to impress you and show you that they have listened to the direction that you have set forth in order to make you proud and it should because that's the true mark of a good leader.

Being Number One

Everybody wants to be number one. Think about it, do you really want to be number one. Do you really want to be the guy or girl that takes all of the glory and all of the criticism when things go wrong and the number one head is on the chopping block? I found in my many years in management It's always good to be the number two or number three to the one that actually gets things done that the number one relies on. You are shielded from the criticisms of being a number one so if you are a person that likes to get things done without the criticism and you're really not a glory Monger, try to be that person that the number one relies on and you will have just as much power as being in the number one spot. There's one thing that i know in my years in management, people at the top surround themselves with smart people and people that make them look better but no matter how much you do or how well you work, they still have to deal with their own demons and a lot of times that's what brings them down. So you can support your number one as much possible, but at the end all of your good deeds and good work won't be the overall cause of their failure so beware of being number one.

Cater Your Instructions

You would not believe how much time people waste given instructions to people, just for them to get it all wrong. It will frustrate you and give you a negative perception of that person or persons that you're trying to give instructions to when they totally get it wrong. This is why you need to cater your instructions to whoever you're trying to get to do the task that you need them to do. Example, if you have one of your employees that is very talkative, I mean a person that never met a conversation that he didn't like to have, you don't want to put this person in a room or have them work with somebody in close quarters because they will spend a lot of time talking. This person you will have to give them Specific instructions, what time frame what they need to do,and benchmarks they need to make. The same task you could give another person you can be totally vague and just say I need this done, but with a person that is very talkative they will spend a minute here a minute there and will literally cost you half an hour to an hour in the long run. Know the majority of your audience as much as you possibly can to cater your instructions in a way that they will understand it without being too cynical. This is easier to do in a one-on-one conversation rather than in a group. Try to get intune with your staff, you would know how far you can go with each group or demographic of people. This is one of the very hard to learn secrets of a very good leader. If you can master that, your on your way to be great at what you do because communicating effectively is the gift that keeps on giving.

SOMETHING IMPORTANT TO TAKE INTO ACCOUNT WHEN GIVING INSTRUCTIONS

❖ The formulations should be short, easy to understand and precise.

❖ To attract the attention of a group, try clapping your hands or knocking on a desk.

❖ The spoken instructions are not everything. The body language counts as well, the gestures, miming etc.

❖ Instructions should always be followed by demonstration. The best way to tell students how to do something is to actually do it yourself.

Praise

It's a very discouraging thing to work very hard and not get recognition for it most people love to praise themselves for doing a very good job. It's really hard to be somber and Quiet when you have done great things you want people to know about it. There's only one problem with that, in my view vanity it's a sin. Yes it is a sin, and i will explain to you why. God gives people talent, people give you praise. Let me say that again " God gives you talent, people give you praise". That talent God gives you is always yours whether you use it or you don't people are the ones that make you famous and give you praise that's why he created us. God cannot praise himself, he created every man, woman, and everything on this planet. It was a very good accomplishment, but without anyone to notice it other than him, he can only give himself a pat on the back how gratifying is that? So we were created to appreciate his good work and praise him for it. So when you do a very good thing or have a major accomplishment know that they never go unnoticed by other people. The bosses may take most of your credit, just find some comfort in knowing that when you've done something great in your work it will show when it's time for you to get your review or your raise. Trust me, when the people who take your credit know you deserve the credit and will give it to you. Unlike your talent that you will half forever, praise comes and goes. So it is up to you to stay focused on doing your good deeds, your life, your work and not get sidetracked with the praise.

Dumb It Down ?????

Dumb it down I've heard this phrase before , but what does it mean? Does it mean if you are surrounded by dumb people be as dumb as they are, or does it mean talk down to them in a dumb way that they can understand. It can be taken both ways, but dumbing it down can be as simple as using small vocabulary words rather than big vocabulary words. Those big words that mean the same as a small word such as adheres, which means the same thing as complies. Or it can be as simple as a phrase like saying, Jack, I need you to express better time management skills, which really means, I need you to work harder or do more in less time. One sounds better than the other and one will get you tangible results and the other one will get you less results. I have never been a big fan of dumbing it down, I would rather bring my employees up and expect more from them because if you consistently have to dumb down eventually this is all you will be doing is dumbing it down and you will find yourself just being dumb and down so if you want to use big words and sophisticated phrases so be it . After all, that's what separates you from them. The other part of dumb it down is when people think that you are very smart and sophisticated. They tend to dislike you without even knowing you and when people are out to get you they will undermine you. People will come at you a lot harder when they think that you are extra smart. They tend to come at you in more sophisticated ways, but wouldn't it be easier to let them come at you in a dumb easy to defend ways. This way you can see it coming and be able to stop it and laugh to yourself. Sometimes dumbing it down can be used like a bulletproof vest, just find that balance between dumbing it down and, not let yourself be dumb and down!

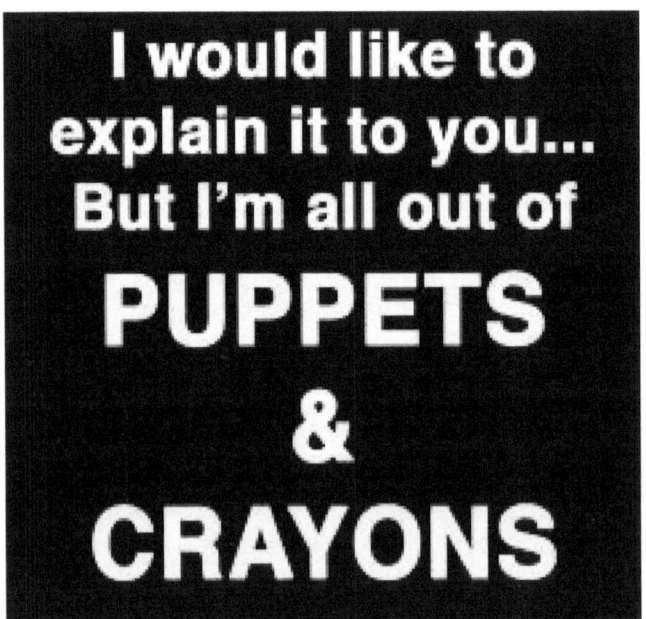

Special To Them

When people do extraordinary things sometimes people try to use them as a model or try to use them as a false goal. Sometimes things are just special to people and cannot be duplicated, unless by more special people. Everybody is not special, even though we live in a world where everything is politically correct, nobody wants to hurt anyones feelings. We all admire and respect greatness, but everyone cannot be great. You cannot compare Michael Jordan to Lebron James two totally different players. One is an exceptionally special person and one is just a good basketball player. If you know anything about basketball I don't have to tell you who the exceptional person is. Tom Brady a very special person who does very special things, you cannot compare other people to him. These are one in a generation people who do once in a generation things. Yes, you can aspire to be like them, but what you're failing to realize is that people like Tom Brady, Michael Jordan or even the Williams sisters are exceptional. They all knew going in that the only thing that really pays off is hard work. So how do we translate that into our day-to-day life in leadership? Don't set benchmarks based on what other people do that is special or exceptional. If you have a person that's sold one million dollars in sales in a week, for example, that might be something that was never accomplished in your company and might not ever be accomplished again, but that might be special to that person. So what you don't want to do is say be like that person because all you do is set people up to fail. Sometimes people are just great at something, people do extraordinary things that cannot be matched. Recognizing that there would never be another Michael Jordan, Tom Brady or the Williams sisters, we might not see people like that in our lifetime. But, if you strive to be just good sometimes you might end up being great, but if you strive to be great and fail you wind up doing more damage than good. So don't hold yourself or other people to expectations that only a very few special people can accomplish, know your limitations, know your strengths, set reasonable goals, and reasonable expectations for you and your staff or the people.

The Kiss Ass Gene

Basically the kiss ass gene is the ability that most people have to kiss ass whenever they can, whether it's kissing their bosses ass, kissing their spouses ass, or kissing their employees ass just to get along is that a good thing? or is it a bad thing? For strong-willed people they lack the kiss ass gene, as if it Stunts their growth in life, relationships, and work. People who work very hard tend to think that their high work ethic is all that matters. They work hard so they don't have to kiss ass, you would be wrong. I learned this fact hard in life myself. I worked vigorously every day to accomplish more than what any other person did push myself to reach higher and higher goals to be a perfectionist, but as long as there is someone above you in a higher position you have to get along with them. Sometimes kissing a little ass will work harder for you and pay off more at times so it's not a bad thing to cater to your boss or brown nose whatever you want to call it, because nobody wants just anyone on their team. That gives the impression that they are stuck up, and that they are better than everybody else. Even if you are, you have to bite the bullet and get along because it pays in the long run.

Put It All Together

All the chapters in the book are things that you will encounter in your life as a leader. A lot of the things in this book, you might have already known. It might just be a additional validation to some of the things that you already know. I might have talked about some things that you didn't know, that's why we stay learning. So when you put it all together, you will become a highly successful leader in whatever field you are in because all of these things are the Ingredients to a successful leader. If you include everything in the recipe, you will be guaranteed a success period . No, it will not be easy but if you are highly focused, you can make it look easy. Remember, it all goes back to repetition doing things the same way over and over and over again. Focus your mind and stay on point with all things. Slowly but surely you will become great, and great things come to great people. Unleash your best self and it will be good for you and the world because if every leader was the best leader they could be this entire world would run like a fine-tuned machine. I also hope you enjoyed reading the book and spending some time with me just to give you a little insight on me I've been in management for over 35 years at the time of me writing this book. I've been that shop steward for local unions. I've been in management of various company's. I currently own four U.S. patents and own two small businesses of my own, so I do use everything in his book in my own life. And lastly when I was very young in management I used to read tips on how to be an effective leader and a lot of the books in those days were very misleading. They almost told you to be godlike over your employees. They used to say things like your employees had nothing good to say, that they couldn't do anything unless they were told to and, their thinking was if they were better than they were then they would be you. During my journey, I found that people are good, that they have a lot of good things to say, it just that they don't want to be leaders. They don't want to be the focus of attention and have to worry about everybody else They just want to worry about themselves. Another misleading way of thinking is that you have to hold all the secrets to yourself so that you will be the only person that knows everything and that makes you valuable so that everyone needs you and never share information. This I also found to be very false because if the people around you are purposely kept down without the proper knowledge, when it's time for you to leave the whole system falls apart. I've actually seen companies in my lifetime go out of business and just disappear altogether for just that reason. Whatever company you work for whether it's a multi-billion-dollar company or a small mom-and-pop place one thing is for sure the name of the business is not the business each employee under your leadership is the business. The more you put into your people the more you are putting into your business and if you don't put anything into your people that is exactly what you will get out of your business.

www.ingramcontent.com/pod-product-compliance
Lightning Source LLC
Chambersburg PA
CBHW051217220526
45473CB00003B/1075